LET'S CELEBRATE

George Washington

and Presidents' Day

by Dorothy and Thomas Hoobler
pictures by Ronald Himler

Silver Press

Produced by Kirchoff/Wohlberg, Inc.
Text copyright © 1990 Kirchoff/Wohlberg, Inc.
Illustrations copyright © 1990 Ronald Himler and
Kirchoff/Wohlberg, Inc.

Published by Silver Press, a division of Silver Burdett Press, Inc.
Simon & Schuster, Inc., Prentice Hall Bldg., Englewood Cliffs, NJ 07632

Printed in the United States of America

10   9   8   7   6   5   4   3   2

Library of Congress Cataloging-in-Publication Data
Hoobler, Thomas.
George Washington and Presidents' Day / by Thomas and Dorothy
Hoobler: pictures by Ronald Himler.
p. cm.—(Let's celebrate)
Summary: Discusses the life and accomplishments of George
Washington and why he deserves to be recognized on Presidents' Day.
1. Washington, George, 1732-1799—Juvenile literature.
2. Presidents—United States—Biography—Juvenile literature.
3. Presidents' Day—Juvenile literature. [1. Washington, George,
1732-1799. 2. Presidents. 3. Presidents' Day.] I. Hoobler,
Dorothy. II. Himler, Ronald, ill. III. Title. IV. Series.
E312.66.H66 1990
973.4'1' 092—dc20   89-49537
[B]   CIP
[92]   AC
ISBN 0-671-69114-7   ISBN 0-671-69108-2 (lib. bdg.)

George Washington

and Presidents' Day

Young George

"Come in, George," said George Washington's mother. "We must talk." She frowned as George walked onto the rug. "Your shoes are muddy. You're eleven years old now. You should know better."

George looked down with surprise. "I'm sorry," he said. "I was down by the river."

His mother shook her head. He was such a wild boy. How would she ever bring him up to be a gentleman?

"You will have to set a better example for your brothers, George. Now that your father is dead, you are the man of the house."

"We'll get along, Mother," George said. "We can still live here on Ferry Farm, can't we?"

"Yes," she said. "But I'm afraid you cannot go to school in England next year."

George smiled. "That doesn't matter. I want to be a farmer. I have enough schooling for that."

His mother wagged her finger at him. "Someday, you will be more than a farmer."

"Being a farmer in Virginia is enough for me," George said. "Can I go fishing now?" His mother smiled and shook her head.

6

One day George was visiting his half-brother Lawrence. "I love it here at Mount Vernon," George said. He looked at the soft green fields and smiled.

Lawrence had become like a father to George.

"You are fourteen now," said Lawrence. "You must think of what you will do in life."

Lawrence took a wooden box from the closet. He handed it to George. Inside the box were shiny metal tools. There were a compass, a chain, and a metal ruler.

"These surveyor's tools belonged to our father," Lawrence said. "He wanted you to have them."

George took the box of tools home. He learned how to use them. He wanted to be a surveyor. As a surveyor, George would measure land and make maps.

The next spring, a farmer told George he was going to plant turnips in a field. "I can survey your field. Then you'll know how much seed to buy," George said.

George did a good job, and the farmer told people about it. Some of them asked George to survey their land. He began to make money as a surveyor.

One day, Lawrence told George some happy news. "I have a surprise for you, George," said Lawrence.

"Let me guess," George said. "You are going to be married. Whom have you chosen? Who will be your bride?" asked George all at once.

Lawrence laughed. "You guessed my surprise. I am going to marry Anne Fairfax."

The wedding was at Mount Vernon. At the wedding, George spoke to Lord Fairfax. He was the head of the Fairfax family. "You should go into the English Navy," Lord Fairfax told George. "I will send you to England. One day you can become the captain of a great ship."

Lawrence agreed with Lord Fairfax. But George's mother did not. "I need him to run the farm," she said.

George was not too disappointed. He liked being a farmer. He liked being at home.

A few months later, a new horse arrived at the farm. It was too wild to ride. "I'll ride him," said George. He saddled the horse and got on.

People stopped working to watch. The horse tried its best to throw George. But George hung on.

The battle went on for hours. Finally, the horse gave up. George could not be thrown.

"If that horse can't throw George, how can I ever control him?" his mother said.

Lord Fairfax did not forget George. One day he sent for him. "I want you to make a survey of some of my land," he said. "It's in the Ohio Valley. You'll have to cross the Blue Ridge Mountains to get there." This time, George's mother let him go.

George had to cross wild country. Only French trappers and Indians lived there. They didn't bother George. But he knew they could be trouble.

When he returned, he gave his maps to Lord
Fairfax. "What will you do with these?" George asked.

"I'll use the maps to divide the land into farms,"
Lord Fairfax said.

"What about the French and the Indians?" asked
George.

"If they make trouble, the king will send his army.
That land belongs to England."

Three years later, Lawrence became ill. He wanted to go to a warm place to get better. George loved his brother. So he went with him. They went to the island of Barbados.

The warm weather did not make Lawrence better. Shortly after he came home, he died.

George never forgot him. He kept a painting of Lawrence next to his desk for as long as he lived.

Lawrence had been in charge of the small army in Virginia. George took his place and became an army major. He was only twenty years old. Many of the soldiers he led were older than he.

The French and Indian War

Lord Fairfax called for George again. "The French and the Indians won't let the English farm in the Ohio Valley," he said. "So we're going to fight them. We need your help. You can show the English soldiers the paths across the mountains."

The war against the French and the Indians began. In one battle, the English general was hit by a bullet. George rode to rescue him. Many men were killed. George led the rest to safety. Later, he found four bullet holes in his clothes. But he wasn't hurt.

The English Army won the French and Indian War. England ruled the eastern part of America.

George was now the owner of Mount Vernon. After the war, he returned there. He married Martha Custis, a young widow with two children. George was content and happy. He loved being a farmer again.

George and Martha had many parties at Mount Vernon. Friends came from all over Virginia. They enjoyed listening to George talk about his adventures. They would gather around him when the dancing ended.

"Tell us about the war," people said. "You were a hero."

"Those days are over," George said. He didn't think he would ever have to fight again. But he was wrong.

First in War

Because the English ruled the land, Americans had to pay taxes to England. They didn't think it was fair to pay taxes to a land so far away. "American tax money should stay in America," they thought. Some Americans said, "We should have our own country."

They decided to fight England. They began to build an army. "Washington should be our general," people said. "He knows how to lead an army."

George wrote a letter to Martha. "I didn't want to accept," he said. "But I could not turn down my friends."

George knew the Americans faced a hard fight. England's army was much bigger than America's.

After two years, the Americans were losing. They had won a few battles. But the English had won more.

Washington's army camped at Valley Forge in Pennsylvania for the winter. His men had to live in tents. "We're freezing," they told the general. "We have no warm clothes. Some of us don't even have shoes."

Every day, Washington talked to the men. "Remember why we're fighting," he said. "We want our freedom. Next year will be better. We can't give up now."

That summer, Washington's army marched south. They headed for Yorktown, Virginia. "We have to move fast," Washington said. "The English Army is camped at Yorktown. We will set up our cannons around the town. That way, we will trap the English."

Finally, the English general gave up. His men marched out of Yorktown. They put their swords down in front of Washington. The war was over.

One of Washington's officers wrote a letter to him. "You should be the king now," he said. "The army would stand behind you."

Washington called a meeting. No one knew why.

"You can see," he said, "how my hair has turned gray from fighting. Now I am almost blind as well.

"We fought to be free," Washington said. "We need no more kings in America. Go home now. Our job is done. The war is over."

First in Peace

Washington went home to Mount Vernon. Soon after, a letter arrived. "Read it for me," George said to Martha.

"They want you to come to Philadelphia," she said. "People are meeting to write laws for the new country. They want you to lead the meeting."

"I can't write laws," he said. "I can't even spell. I'm needed here at the farm."

Martha smiled. "Your country needs you, George," she said. She knew he would go.

Washington traveled to Philadelphia. The meeting there lasted all summer. People didn't agree about the new laws. They said, "Let's find out what Washington thinks." The people knew he was wise and fair.

Finally, they wrote a plan. It was called the Constitution. We still live under its laws today.

The Constitution said a president should be the head of the United States. Each of the thirteen states sent men to choose the president.

When the votes were counted, all of them were for George Washington. Everyone cheered, except George. He wanted to return to his farm and his family. But he agreed to be the first president of the United States.

George Washington was president for eight years. When his term as president was over, he was very happy. Once again, he could return to Mount Vernon. Once again, he could be a farmer.

Farming was always what George Washington loved best. But he put his country's needs above his own. In return, Americans have always loved their first president.

One of his generals had said Washington was "First in war, first in peace, and first in the hearts of his countrymen." That is how we remember him.